On the Outside Looking up

Joshua Turek

On the Outside Looking Up

© Joshua Turek 2024

Cover Art by Arooj
Based on a photograph by
Isabelle Barrymore

for more info on author visit:
www.joshuaturek.com
@joshuaturek

To Siobhan

The Folly

Nature's Simp

I'm not throwing shade at people
who dress casual to go hiking,
But I just revere nature so much
it demands formal attire.

And I'm no pick me bitch either,
I'm no simp.

I just know how to treat a lady,
and by "lady" I mean Mother Nature.

So I guess you could say I'm
a bit of a MILF hunter. Mother I'd Like to Frolic
upon.

How sublime to bask in—
what was that?!

"Brother!"

"We all choose our different paths."

"Wait!"

Catcall From the Heart

God I just saw the finest fucking girl walk by
and I thought I was gonna yell something at her
but I didn't.
I only thought to myself,
God is it such a fucking miracle
that two people with wildly different
experiences, hopes and dreams
ever find one another at all.
And how love must be the great reducer of Ego
that allows us to see ourselves as less separate from one
another.
And then she kept walking almost out of sight
and I thought…
My God does she have a nice ass.
But I didn't say it.
I only thought it.
I only thought it!
I only catcalled my own heart.

Marathon Man

Do you ever feel like to make ends meet,
you're helping the world, meet its end?

I sell used cars and times have never been better,
we're raking in the cash,
but you wanna know a secret?

I don't even own a car.

I walk off this lot,
the 26.2 miles to my home.
Stop on off at a McDonald's
and bribe one of the drivers to
buy me my Big Mac meal from the late night Drive-Thru
because they won't serve you on your feet,
They want you in their machines,
and I don't want to be a cog in the machine I'm a human
being.

So as the Colorado River dries up
and Yosemite burns, I walk
and not just because I got a DUI during my divorce
and my license was suspended.

I walk to spend time with Mother Earth,
gently, tenderly,
like you would with any sick relative.

So…

If you're looking for a new
or pre-owned vehicle,
get in touch.

I'm not like other car salesmen.

Back to the Office

Tech Workers this is your founder and CEO
and "Guru" if you so choose. It's time to come back
to the office now. Yes, studies have shown working from
home has actually increased your productivity and made
you happier. But you see, I was a lonely adolescent and I
did not start this company to be neglected of the attention I
now deserve. You see, as workers you are irreplaceable to
witnessing me being a maverick, founder and CEO in our
open office floor plan. Who is going to write my biography
if there are none to speak of my unorthodox some would
say genius ways as I meander through our open office floor
plan? Come back to the office we got kombucha on tap!
Come back! Why work at home and be near your loved
ones when you can be close to those who catalyze and
inspire you? It's time to get back into the office
now, I'm nothing without you!

I Love Dinner Parties

I'm considering polyamory
so that my partner and I
have a few more lovers
to lay in bed with
despairing about the state of the world
as tears silently trickle
down our faces.
Yes, that's right
I'm considering polyamory
to have more intimates to hate the world with.
I don't know what the term for that is, *Polyhatory*?
Personally I just think it's unnatural
to expect only one person
to contain all your bitterness.
To not only see me naked
but also have to endure
my existential dread
after the endorphin rush dreaminess of the post coital
afterglow fades,
and the crushing weight of capitalism returns.

Work Must Go On

Gen Z really thought getting face tattoos
would prevent them from having to get normal jobs.
But Millennials are the middle managers now
and we're open minded as fuck.

We'll even throw in a face tattoo as your signing bonus
if you come fold clothes for us at the Levis store on the 3rd
Street Promenade.

Oh no, we must keep shoveling coal into this furnace.
These student loans aren't going to pay themselves.
In fact, if you ever get margaritas with us after work
sometime, maybe we'll show you the tramp stamps we got
back in '05, Cancun Spring Break, Cisqo was playing that
Thong Song, things were electric, we didn't have to worry
about social media!

Listen, we didn't want these jobs either.
Until we start the revolution,
you're going to have to suffer with us.
And we can talk about our therapists together.

You're hired!

Sensitive Type

Saw the movie Free Willy in theaters with my great aunt
Carol when I was a boy and on our way out she asked
which one of us kids cried during the movie and I was the
only one who admitted it, so she told me I got to ride
shotgun on the way home

and I've been crying to get my way ever since.

San Pedro

People wanna know why the supply chain is breaking down? It's because workers like me are breaking down! I just had my hours cut, on purpose mind you. I don't wanna be out there loading crates for Amazon. You know what I really wanna do? I wanna write poems. I wanna read Carl Jung and Sigmund Freud and explore the endless depths of the human experience. And you can't do that out there, on the docks. You do that in your heart, you do that in your head. The supply chain's breaking down because we're breaking down, we're breaking down our walls. A great softening is occurring . And maybe that's not such a bad thing.

(goes to toss helmet into the ocean dramatically only to reveal it's still in his hand)

I wouldn't actually throw that in the water I'm not a litter bug. I love nature and plan to spend more time in it from now on.

Topanga Living Cafe

People in L.A. are always going on and on about how much
they love nature
and how centered they feel here.
Yeah, yeah, as long as I'm on a groomed trail
with my manmade equipment
to ensure my dominion over nature,
there's nothing better.
But you get me three feet off of this hiking trail
and it's man versus nature,
kill or be killed,
and I have every intention of using my wits
and my technology
to come out on top.
Because I will get back to my Toyota Prius
and go buy a blueberry smoothie with lavender in it.
Yeah, they put lavender in smoothies now in L.A.
and it's good.
I bet you didn't even know you could drink em like that?
You can.
And if nature wants to try to stop me?
That's when I get my pocket knife out.

Namaste.

Detective Music

Moms are always like
"Why don't you come live with me?"

Because I'm 35.
I should have kids of my own by now.

Do I? No.

Am I taking a poetry class at a community college?

Yeah!

Oceanica

Are you tired of smelling like a lie?
Finally! A fragrance that mirrors your soul!

Emptiness

The very first cologne with nothing in it.
An absence of hope is not just a vibe,
it's a scent.
There is no message in this bottle either,
only a dance partner with the void,
a hollowed out companion unfed by longing.

But what if a different scent awakened you?
A calling from your ancestral home?

We came from the sea,
our bodies still carry its tides within
and so we shall return.

To find salvation in what we already are:
soaking wet miracles who reek of this watery globe,
we never smell alone.
Never. Smell. Alone.
Oceanica by Joshua Turek
Why be empty?
When you can be full of it.

Clothesline

I ask my neighbor Valerie about the clothesline,
she says she doesn't mind,
my neighbor Valerie suggests if her husband
isn't home,
that I smell her drying brasserie.

My neighbor Valerie,
mon cherie,
she who trusts me to be discreet,
this is just between her and me.
Like lightning the way two flowers meet.
Oh, how I cherish my returns from the bodega
down the street.

Never mind a bachelor like me.
I raise a glass to a neighbor like her.
Thank you for being so generous
with your laundry.

Suburbs Into the Sea

Do you believe in love at first swipe?
You know, online dating and all that.

She said, we could be the King and Queen
of Sunken City baby.

Maybe I should've asked her
what she meant by that?

Guess I got so excited at the thought
of ruling over something.

Got caught up thinking love
makes royalty of us.

How we lord it over icy mountains and
hot volcanoes.

And for awhile love is
victory against even pain.

I guess I should've asked her last name though.
All I had was her match.

Now it seems like maybe she deleted
her profile.

The Great Reducer of Ego

That About You

Citrus trees full of unpicked fruit
and my single friend's longing.

I don't want to be in a power couple
I want to be in a poem couple where we
write each other poems.

Never learned how to love
I had to learn how to love.

I remember first saying I love you.
Driving through strawberry fields,
You know I love you right?
We say it cuz we run out of things to say love to.
First when you're beginning,
it's I love kissing you.
      the way you smell.
      your mind.
      the way you interpret life. Shit I love you don't I?

Abalone Point Campground #1

Up and down the Pacific Coast
stalked by blackberries.
From Santa Cruz to Bellingham
they followed us everywhere we camped.

It was the pandemic summer
when we sought escape.
They burst in your mouth with sweet salinity by the ocean
just before the Redwoods towered over us.

In Northern Washington my mom said the best ones
were next to the highway.
She was right, they tasted
like the open road feels.

My little sister had her freshman year of college
sent back from the dorms to home.
I had nowhere to be so I followed the fruit
as it followed me.

My girlfriend made a blackberry cobbler of utter perfection
out of the ones we'd all collected.
Me and the girls, us and our
time.

I hope we look back on what we did,
stalked by all that's grown along our path,
knowing we tangled in our directions
with it.

Dogfather

My wife wanted a dog, so I put my foot down and
then I put my other foot down and said ok.

Now, I'm the one who takes him out.
Three to four miles both morning and night,
sandwiching the rest of my life in between.
Only sometimes, I wonder if this is actually my life, being
with my dog,
and the rest of the stuff are just things I have to do?

Also, I didn't want the dog but then within ten minutes of
meeting him,
we were licking each other's faces.
It was a lot like being on the dance floor of a nightclub in
your early 20's,
just like "I don't know who you are beautiful stranger, but I
want to spend the rest of my life with you."

Here we are living our lives together
me and this 12 pound poodle
I outweigh him by about 200 pounds.

Wi Spa

Had our 7 yr anniversary yesterday
its fascinating how when we first fall in love
we start memorizing every inch
then as we grow
it becomes about unlearning
and the novelty in understanding
so much mystery to the whole thing
and how amazing the awe

belly rubs

love is just like hey would i
show my stomach to that person on any sort of regular
basis?
and would they appreciate the presence of my stomach?
and that's it,
two people walking around the apartment with our
stomachs out,
feeling safe and loved
stomach to stomach.

Highlands

Sometimes I come up here to mourn how
the patriarchy stripped me of my ability
to do just that.

Bell Hooks says boys are only allowed to express an
emotion if it's anger.

I swear it's like the world is just looking for a reason to call
me a little bitch. I'm not btw. I'm 6'5 220lbs so if anything
I'd be a big bitch.

Which, as you can see, I'm not btw.

Liver King says you have to dominate your environment. I
get his point but if I'm being honest:

I want to use my strength to survive and enjoy my life. I
don't need to conquer anyone.

So I keep walking until I'm tired enough to feel the fight
leaving my bones.

And I surrender to my weakness. Catching a glimpse of
who I am without all these muscles.

Without this raw masculinity.

Bell Hooks says within the word masculinity is the word "mask". I mean the spelling's not right but I get what she's saying.

I'm willing to acknowledge I'm wearing one. That I am afraid of what's beneath.

Yeah, that's right, I'm afraid. Fear, that's the emotion right before anger.

So I guess I'm up to at least two emotions now. Hey, a man's gotta start somewhere, right?

A Pantoum to Fill a Room

This is how you explained it to me on our knees
that you had never prayed for a miracle
but wrote a signed letter in your heart to God,
switched into lotus pose for a transmission of thought.

That you had never prayed for a miracle,
in a life lived off stage while raging like a performer,
switched into lotus pose for a transmission of thought,
how our desire is to merely be an illusion confirmed.

In a life lived off stage you raged like a performer.
We met as your fires blazed uncontained.
How our desire is to merely be an illusion confirmed,
it's why we were indistinguishable from my place to yours.

We met as your fires blazed uncontained,
1920's studios along the same beat up strip of pain
It's why we were indistinguishable from my place to yours,
bed bugs, flooded sinks, laundromats and creaky floors.

1920's studios along the same beat up strip of pain
Slumlord tenants we met in the rain
Bed bugs, flooded sinks, laundromats and creaky floors.
You grew up in the church but had never prayed for a
miracle.

Slumlord tenants we met in the rain
got jobs at the same place and felt our way. You grew up in
the church but had never prayed for a miracle.
That's how you explained it without ever saying.

Got jobs at the same place and felt our way
drank coffee, ate pastries, felt love summon itself
that's how you explained it without ever saying,
How our tiles of grief were rearranged into a pane.

Drank coffee, ate pastries, felt love summon itself,
gently melting, tires screeching, horns blaring,
how our tiles of grief were rearranged into a pane,
this is how you explained it to me on our knees.

At the Edge of the Earth

Holding warm hands in those off kilter moments that come
right before
drifting off to sleep,
I had this terrible flash of an urgent voice:
It's all gonna happen so fast.
Saw us in our last years
same as we were in bed,
elderly and tender, falling asleep scared per usual.
This morning,
I awoke strong again and
understanding the goal in life
(that I learned from loving you)
is to allow yourself to turn tender,
as much as your version of God will allow,
maybe that's the gift of old age if we make it there?
To feel your body tenderizing and embracing the feeling
as it aligns with your brave heart tenderizing.

2/13/23

We come to Earth to
suffer and heal.
The healing feels instructive,
to constant pain.
Suffering is converted to healing by effort.
    We lay in bed
after our efforts at conversion
and my bum ankle
feels better than brand new.

Menottis

love seeing those sex stoned
one night stands tumbling out of bed
into morning light deciding to get coffee
at the shop together.
the sun that fork in the road
to lose each other with a little caffeine or hold on
to the curiosity there could be another occasion to follow.
how on ours i said the food at stories bookstore and cafe
was chicken scraps
and she ate a wrap or bagel or something like that and i
wasn't sure it would ever happen again
now life would be unrecognizable
without her

February 28, 2018

A crow squawks, "Hear that? Those are my children,"
my mom says from her bed in the living room of her one
bedroom Mercer Island apartment.

My little sister explained my mom feeds the crows peanuts
from the window next to her bed. Says she dislodges the
window screen to do it.

I'm up here for the first time. My mom and little sister
moved here six months ago sight unseen. My mom found
out she had breast cancer four months later.

She had a double mastectomy yesterday. I drove her home
today, "Home sweet home," she said when she climbed into
bed, a dozen pillows awaiting to brace her.

The surgery went well. "What size breast did they give
me?" She asked not long after we were admitted as visitors
into her Seattle hospital room.

I call my girlfriend back in Los Angeles. We talk about our
moms, I say mine gives me creativity. When I stay open to
her it's the chaos and wonder that's fostered me.

And now here I am drawing closer to middle age, watching
my mother sleep in an apartment near a city I don't know.

When my mom got out of surgery she said her "throat was
dry like the frickin Sahara Desert." When my dad got out of
surgery three years before her he took all the cords and
tubes in front of him and said "Spaghetti". When I told her
that, she admitted he was funny. It's one of two things they
agreed on about him, that he was funny and great at putting
in an I.V.

Drugged, before her surgery yesterday morning sitting
before me in a pre-surgery room with no cell phone service,
my mom told me it wasn't just selfishness that informed
her reasoning for having six kids it was also that she
wanted to make us out of love and joy.

The Grind

Man in the City

I'm just a man in the city.
We don't talk much, me and the other people.
But I like knowing that they're there.
It makes me feel like I'm a little more here.

I suppose being around other people makes me feel a little
more like a person myself. And sometimes I get so down
about my existence it feels like the only hands holding me
up belong to those people out here.

(Who will never actually touch me with their hands and yet
they do touch me)

Ahh, vodka! I suppose a man in the city has to numb
himself one way or another. Or he'd explode from all the
pain he witnesses day to day.

Yet when it does shine through it oddly brings him a little
closer to understanding his own pain.

And after all, maybe a city is just an exponential
phenomenon trying to understand itself faster and harder
because it has more of itself to learn from.

And here I am just talking to myself like men in the city so
often do. Grateful that it's here listening.

Screen Time

The most daring thing you can do these days
is let yourself be bored.
Turn off your screens and just sit there
and tell me it's not a high.
The walls closing in.
The refrigerator hum of your own existence.
It's exhilarating if you ride the fear.
But most of us can't,
we buckle,
seek dopamine
instead of the thrill in self regulating it.
Too bad,
because the terror of this being *it*
is where seeds of enlightenment are found.
Besides, I learned from a numerologist
down at the handball courts of the Venice Boardwalk
that even in our loneliest moments of despair
we're never really alone,
because being alone
is a presence in and of itself.

America Is Not a Melting Pot It's a Blender

Does this grocery store in L.A.
sell a $21 smoothie?

Yeah, they do.

Does that faze me?

Not in the slightest.

A glass of wine at a swanky restaurant
will cost you about the same. And that's only grapes.

This is fruits, berries, and fungi from around the globe.
Married into a compostable cup.When you think about it,
ain't that America? Just a bunch of us (from various parts
of the world) crushed and cut down into this thing together,
that we're working toward and would be so delicious if the
mass of us could actually afford.

But most of us can't. That's why I brought my own soda
from home. Just to look. Just to gaze at the $21 smoothie
of an American dream.

And uh the people here are hot too.

Urgent Care

You can see the HOLLYWOOD sign
from the checkout line
of the Silver Lake Erewhon's
intimidating floor to ceiling windows.
You look through the glass,
while holding grocery items
from the hot food bar,
that only a movie star
can reasonably afford.

Double Double

Don't ever disrespect someone else's Fast Food
preferences.
That shit is deeply personal
and what's inside that warm paper bag has been there for
them in moments
no one else has.
So I respect your Fast Food choices,
I hope you respect mine.
And the world can be a better place.

Illuminati Homes Not Yours Don't Worry

Lately, I've been thinking how security cameras
outside 20 million dollar houses are an admission by the
owners,

they have accrued a disproportionate amount
of resources and now must protect this rotting surplus—

from those unfortunate ones who might be looking to
restore the balance.

How the uber rich become barricaded by
the same crocodiles they put in their moats,

to sever from the mass
to whom they innately belong.

Don't worry, this isn't about you. Nor I! But Jane Jacobs
would be shitting her pants if she knew,

every person lucky to live indoors, not only would be doing
it in a high walled prison box

but have a Ring camera to ensure their
hair conditioner delivery from Amazon

wasn't stolen by a person who showers
at the beach.

We've Always Known You

Is there a story I can honestly tell? Fatigue, spiritual imbalance, a slant to things. Is there a shape to the world I recognize at the moment? I see it in cubes of time. I hear it in loud cries of machines and voices. People coming and going but so often going these days. It's astounding how many people have gone. You can't build affordable housing atop a cemetery. What if you put it on stilts? Let the ghosts hold up the space between earth and units of living. You can't find compromise with a broken ego, desperate not to recognize what it could gain by staying broken.

Wheeler Gorge

It costs so much money to give up on society
and move to the wilderness,
so I'm out here for $33 dollars a night
simulating the experience.

Taking plant medicine to accelerate the healing,
becoming unfrozen,
relocating feelings that would've been my birthright
had generations of men never been infected
with wanting more than they needed.

I wonder if 30 years in the wild would feel like a longer life
than 80 in the modern experience with all its toys
that prolong our time but reduce our meaning?

I wonder if the same would be true living a few days
as a water bug?

Or one crackling campfire, a flicker, a flame, a roar, and
then water lapped ashes.

Y

Have we been too afraid
of stepping on toes?

New technologies, same outcomes, enriched portfolios of
those doing none of the labor, boomer parents, rich infants,
illuminati, whoever.

Why didn't we form something beneficial with our
Myspace top 8's, offline?

Demanded, people pleased, broken boundaries, thrusting
productivity into ourselves like we were trained. Despite
the self awareness, worst part, I'm paralyzed by craving
comfort.

Women, men, they, them, we've been well behaved ones
who aren't making history. My only suggestion is we get
together at public parks and start talking to each other until
they make it illegal and start infecting our tribes with spies.

A Tribute to the Dustbowl

I've been selling you
to anyone who'll hear my story.

There's no beginning, middle, or end.

I've been selling you
in half punch-drunk glory,

I've been writing it all down with my pen.

The sky is just a big black blanket,
the stars,
tears we've shed.

Sometimes I don't think I can take it,
sometimes,
you just won't leave my head.

Oh, I've been selling you.

Pep Talk to Myself After Work

No one
ever
gives you credit for saving
your own life
on a day to day basis,
but every day where you take care of yourself,
you're saving your own life
and it's heroic
make no mistake about it.
No matter how much people discredit you for simply
existing
you're not just existing
you're saving your own life.

Dialogue #6

I know she's not cheating on me because she'd be in a better mood.

Not Another Title

"Make your life matter." It says in cursive sprayed black on
one of many deteriorating RV's in Venice Beach.
Everything is a slogan, the poor emulate corporate
billboards, it's the language we've been taught and how we
think in advertisements and battles of propaganda.
I notice birds too,
little sparrows on post office drop boxes
and black crows elsewhere.
The little birds cant be good omens if the crows aren't bad
ones. Questionable signs and conditioning,
in the depths of a trip we thumbed through Siobhan's bird
book in her Toyota Rav 4
in Malibu Creek State Park parking lot.
The underside of a hawks wings painted in white and
brown like a message,
Oh, the animals are our brothers and sisters!
Despite this evolutionary game of survival with its
temporary winners
there is an understanding if we listen, like how
hummingbirds are my dad because one flew into his house
minutes after he passed. And how
we are visited each day by significance
in a quiet language we already know should we pause to
remember it.

Dialogue #3

I want to start a revolution but I also want to be left alone.

But you're a waiter.

Hey elitist! Are you saying, I can't start a revolution because I'm a waiter?

No, I'm saying they won't leave you alone.

Exhibitionists

Social Media 2014: no one's life can be that perfect

Social Media 2024: no one's life can be this miserable?

It Grows the Economy

Those poor kids in Gaza
those poor kids in Sudan
adults can be sad orphans
adults can be bad men.

The Luxury of Broken Ambition

Jeff Bezos went to Coachella
for his midlife crisis. But
you can't buy the fun you
once had,
when you were young
and promise-less enough
to have it.

That Wistful Vibe

Far West Farms

As a child I fantasized,
about robbing a Coca Cola vending machine,
because one morning I saw its guts.
An open womb with
a uniformed man filling it up.
After school I'd stick my hand up
through its bottom flap,
feeling the possibility of treasure on my fingers.
I think back then, they were only 65 cents?
Those sweet cold cans of relief from the heat.
Another victim of their marketing, how they'd
hit my tongue addiction the
saccharine stimulants to cure childhood of its boredom,
the rumble of the can rolling down the
inner mountain of the machine
a diabetic birth orgasm,
I wanted one
I wanted one free of charge.

The Boys

I've been hanging out with a
lot of my friends from
childhood lately who are
now middle-aged men and
we're all stuck in our
normalish lives but I want to
say to them "Hey don't worry, I remember when
everything we did flickered
with significance and you
are giants to me."

Entrada

Don't fear,
there are only rebirths
to contend with
and water to transport in our cells,
carbon bodies to feed the trees.
You can find our chemical make up
in a hardware store for a reasonable price
but our miracle is sold nowhere.
Here, where I live, the citrus is about to grow
from white flowers,
on winter limbs again,
bringing the Southland back its sour days of hope.

What I Think About

In the California desert before Instagram, my friend and I
climbed sand dunes we'd stumbled upon with no map.
He had once played a Power Ranger on TV,
but trudging up the uncertain surface he confessed he
had to "quit the smokes". I couldn't believe my lungs were
stronger than his, a Power Ranger, he lifted weights in his
room, survived on Pro Max bars and Miller Lites. I thought
he was a legend.

We were looking for the perfect emptiness
to make a movie by ourselves with no money,
but instead found everything in between, atop the dunes we
watched the sun leave
behind a dried lake bed that didn't fit our vision for the
film.

He and I drove all the way to Nevada,
slept in a Motel 6 outside Las Vegas.
Sat in the lonely room eating In N' Out burgers and
drinking their milkshakes,
back when the corn syrup still pinched your throat,
he had the grilled cheese because he was a vegetarian.

He lost his work visa a few months after I lost my mind.
"Alien of Extraordinary Ability"
he told me the visa said and we joked about that,
sometimes I'd keep him company while he got paid cash to
make quesadillas at a dive bar in Culver City behind a big
movie studio. But that was when we were friends.

Eventually I quit on him, withheld use of my camera
because I had to sell it
because I was broke with no cell phone living in
Hollywood behind the mall, not a producer.

He got deported and ended up making a version of the
movie in New Zealand. I've still never seen it but his next
movie after that made him kind of famous. I saw a picture
of him and James Cameron sharing a stage. I haven't seen
him in person since we were so young,

But I sometimes think about how we had a great sense of
humor together. About how he used to joke about wanting
to "break my face" because he had once been a boxer
and how after I mentioned that he sure joked about it a lot,
he stopped telling me he wanted to "break my face" and
then we joked about that confrontation too.

Topanga Nettle Soup

Whatever happened
to the blue bus all you
bedraggled youths used to ride around in?

At dawn of the tech age,
as the minimum wage got so stagnant
no one could hack it.

How did the kids who
never stopped taking pictures ever
find time to remember?

Our skin wasn't thin
it got that way
forgotten in the blender,
dreams died and were reborn
every year one week off in December.

Sat up in the hills staring in
the wrong direction off Mulholland,
cars below looked like glowing saddled slugs
a cross on a hillside,
it felt like a miracle
anytime, anyone
could get anywhere
they were
going.

Without Hesitation We Slurped Spilled Sake Off the Bar Counter

Like how back then,
I used to be more caught up in the mystery.
Did you crane your head down less?
Look into their eyes more?

I remember Jeff with a bundle of night blooming jasmine
flowers
in the strings of his guitar,
singing along to it on Venice Boulevard.

How the booze went too far, chased him through the
fragrant orchards of well to do homeowners, lost his
sprinting body en route to his sister's car, how I
found him standing atop a parking payment machine at the
beach.

I remember dressing normal but feeling like a freak.

Now, late at night beauty incapacitates me,
the breeze feels too beautiful, the moon aches severe, my
lover's eyes shape too gorgeous. I shovel it out of my leaky
canoe in buckets.

Milky Way

Do you remember when we were
on that street in New York City that could have been
anywhere?

Careless 1970's style auto parts stores, liquor marts, and
wide-lane roads. No density or rows of people on the
sidewalk, like in the movies, it was absent any textured
clues that gave hint you and I were in a magical city.

I don't recall how we re-entered that grown ass playground,
beer and a shot special everywhere for five dollars in 2017.
But I think of you and I sitting next to the Teddy Roosevelt
statue on a bench inside the Natural History Museum
having existential meltings.

I mean maybe yours was a little more well-aimed and mine
was just to take a crack at one since we were already on the
subject. But we talked until we felt better, it's possible I
instilled some fantasy of what we could take our ability and
become in place of all that it felt like we weren't,

And we rebounded enough to get shakes at the Shake
Shack near the museum and walk the condensation beaded
plastic cups through Central Park,
as the humidity rolled the sweet lactose in my already
plump gut from the stress eating I'd continued that summer

and we took our time to the public toilets and life serenaded
us.

My Brother's Ex Girlfriend From When They Were in 4th Grade

Her dad sold used Levis
at the bottom of Las Flores Canyon.

We threw ice cubes at the diners
above us on the patio of Moonshadows.

Crawled under beach houses,
feral vermin, the ocean so thick with salt
it smelled like body odor.

Old Lucy once said her dead actor father,
would call the sand the natural land conclusion of the
Western Hemisphere. I say all the time this is where the
malcontents followed the trail of tears, blood, and dead
bison hides and the dissatisfied runners ran out of earth so
they sat here in the sun and dreamed.

She started a big band with a skinny guy you met
downtown sang about home and then they
tried to screw her out of royalties, I heard,
but she was the spirit engine she was the glue
while they huffed something they couldn't alone do.

I saw my childhood friend Aaron who was
briefly a pop star in the dying days of MTV
and even as I talked to him
I don't think he remembered me.

Barbie Dreams

She moved us to a rundown stucco beach house Mice
infested they ate holes through our clothes Shit
in our pantry Salt battered paint
Exhaust blackened windows facing the relentless highway
Inside we were powerfully rocked back and forth by
incoming waves thundering against pillars holding us up
and 46,000 cars per day hemming us in Airplane
turbulence we shook on unsteady feet threw
old sourdough bread for seagulls to catch dive bomb
Our toy poodle Peaches got ran over and killed that first
month
The suicidal rescue German Shepherd Amber leapt
from a balcony 3 stories high onto rocks below I
Remember
one El Niño night it rained and the Mold
freckled skylight above our bunk bed blew off And And
And
I figured on the lower bunk
I could
just stay there under my blanket and Survive
wet shivering under my brother who stayed there above I
Slept
a lot in those days
I would go to sleep early as possible
Wake back up tired like I'd found no peace

Run
across murderous Pacific Coast Highway with my sister
Britt Holding
hands when there was Enough Enough Enough
lapsed time between hurtling cars Pay
$1.35 for 434 bus pockets full of scrounged pennies
sometimes Sometimes Once in awhile
he'd let us on without our fare Gray
beard the bus driver had a gray beard as my own
starts to pale in that direction I survived
grew up Started remembering younger things in pieces
which threaded into me as I rotated through time
and an important thing to grasp about a thread
is that for the strand to continue in its strengthening First
it must disappear and Rise
back up with a Faith that it first went to another side.

Petrified Forest

Big Macs in bed
at the Holbrook, Arizona, Days Inn
sauce on our chins,
lettuce jumping out in four directions
with every bite.
The pastel colors of the petrified landscapes we saw earlier,
a blue sky, the bright light
silence thick, an absence of life.

Attending to the inner details of objects
in a motel room belonging to
a mundane part of America.
Not everything has to entertain us,
nestled in our thoughts and their $100 a night rooms
like ants crawling across earth
In N' Out of what we can dream up.

The dazzling sunset outside room 225
stucco arc framed like the M in McDonalds
finishing of the day,
a cold town water tower backdropped by scattered flame.

The planet is lonely without life animating it,
sacrificing for each other to carry on.

Benito hated the death of that long ago Terra Firma,
how without us,
the planet's cradling crust would hold nobody up,
rings of time would go uncounted,
water wouldn't have Triassic tree trunks
to pour itself into and then crystalize
and be observed.

Paramount Studios

In Hollywood,
there are no ends.
Something always happens,
again and again.

A love affair,
gone wrong. One
of those depressions
lasting too long.

The night was slow,
My friend got stoned.
His dog saw a ghost,
stood up on her toes.

He showed me the vid,
of her in the room.
Looking real scared.
Barking at the air.

A Dog.

A God.

A Fear.

You can tell
there's someone there.

Line

Trust the nonsense,
there appears to be less life in the desert
so that which you recognize takes on a significance.

If you arrived by boat into Marina Del Rey
and wanted to hallucinate in nature
you'd fork right to the desert or left up the coast.

You'd be correct to do either.
In the desert where yellow butterflies splatter the
windshield
on their migration like being hit with a gentle paintball but
you are
murderous road trippers.

In Ojai where the pink moment sunsets
set the air aglow at Wheeler Gorge
we didn't know what was happening
until I remembered the wifi password at the motel
"Pink Moments" they have them because of the
atypical direction the mountains go

Then I undercooked the hamburgers on the grill
and Christian said "You made another pink moment".

July 17, 2021

I haven't
seen my friend
in awhile.
Not since
awhile back when he
passed by me with pink hair and a mask.

He locks up his phone
in a vault timed to kidnap
his technology addiction
so he can have time
to think longer about his own existence.

Of late I have felt,
I never see my friends
offline or in my periphery,
they're splattered about my heart and
laced up into knots of memory
but out here nowhere to be found.

I bet if I saw him again
at the library or wandering up and down Sunset Blvd.,
he'd say something about some current preoccupation
he has been turning over in his mind or whatever
that would connect my thought of the moment
to a new branch of his.

Green Notebook

We'll be making mince meat
of the sky, before long.
I feel hydrogen, smell carbon,
see bubbles of oxygen, taste testosterone.
The blood of the lamb, a butcher's paradise,
jail sentence, prison break,
there are fates we are born into
and fates we can't escape.
Sunshine on a cold lake.
Sunshine on a dewy blade.
The rotten moon an eaten apple core,
a threat of mercury, blazing temperatures,
dried marijuana, apricots, skin,
peel me open like an Ojai pixie tangerine,
towel me off like a senior living patient.
I am gummy, I'm a spade,
a sharp knife, a mistake.
Summer spears into us until we're changed.

Off Hillcrest

The people who bought my dad's condo
after he died, tracked me down
to tell me an old photograph of mine
randomly appeared in their garage.

So I drove out to the Conejo Valley,
like I had so many times when he was alive,
from my life in the city,
and I picked myself up.

It was a mystery, they said. How my photo
just appeared after five years of them living there.
A big three foot poster board of a blonde child at two years
old, in a black cowboy hat on a toy horse.

No idea how they missed something that big or how we
did, moving his stuff out years before in the adrenaline of
shock.

That's when it's best to clean out a loved ones
belongings btw, when the death is too recent to process
the preciousness of their stored away batteries they'd
never use in devices they didn't need anymore.

On the way home I took myself to the first beach
I ever went to. My dad thought birds were signs
from the Universe. I watched them fly past me in
slow motion, three foot tall image, nearby on the sand.

Spring in Hell

A living squirrel at the cemetery
climbing over memories.
Clusters of baby ones
at the park,
rolling around the grass
like billiard balls.

I'm alive in percentages,
gaslit by technology.
Fully charged,
gathering near strangers but alone
exploring ourselves.

Silence taunts us in the city
between swirling helicopter blades
churning their blue butter in the sky.

Rumbling garbage trucks slamming
dumpsters onto the pavement of
back alleys beneath our bedroom windows.
The neighbors making love loud enough
to remind the rest of us
listening that we aren't,
but once had on magnetic days.

Birthblade

I turn 37 today.
Before I got inline skates
a guy wearing them told me
they'd be great for my love life.
Something about building
up your muscles in all the right places.
Even if you don't get any style points for wearing them.
My dad passed when I was 30,
so it hasn't been easy growing up
without a father, is my joke.
He put me in charge of the family cell phone plan and
there was almost a mutiny against me.
A couple of my siblings wanted to upgrade
phones but I urged caution in their grief.
They got em anyway and were fine.
I think maybe I'd been projecting my
own instability. It was sort of like a lower-middle class
version of that HBO show Succession.
Anyway, the point is I'm a man now and
life is good. I live, laugh, love, just like
the bumper sticker says to do. I stand on
my own eight wheels. My shadow merges in
gratitude with the physical. I get visited by
butterflies and that's more than enough.

fred the landlord

my brother and i watched a man
die together.

that man just so happened to be
our father.

there were other witnesses too but imo:

none of them inched as
close to the wreckage as he and i did.

we were so close the medicine was practically
in our blood.

the ports in our chests.

you may not believe me.

but when my dad was sick with
cancer my brother went to the ER
more times, suffering
from many symptoms but
ultimately a broken heart.

———

my brother and i lived together for
much of our 20s.

i spent my 20s
living in venice beach with him where i
learned nothing.

there, with my
brother.

hanging on for dear life
and goofing around, fighting the sounds
of leaf blowers and barking dogs and
never having money, never having money.

i remember the first day we moved
in he asked "now what?" i told
him this is where we grab our
laptops and go to the coffee shop.
and that's what we did. that's what
he still does and so do i.

———

my brother and i lived in santa
monica together in our earlier 20s.
the lady next door hated us
because we acted hateable.

before that we briefly lived in the valley,
there was a little man who roamed
the parking garages, we called him
tsar nicholas.

————

my brother and i shared a room when
we were kids. we used to make our family laugh
at the dinner table. my brother
eating his piece of meat like a
caveman. i follow, grunting, a clueless
neanderthal, tearing at
the meat. family roaring in
laughter, the only way to take
that edge of emotion
running through the house
and juggle our steak knives with it.

————

he brought me back to my dad. said
the guy missed me.
how our family never could speak
directly until we were old enough
to fail at it ourselves. the middle
man. a middle child always
able to see through our
parents and probably me, his brother.

how to be strong. my brother and i,
were always looking for ways to
be strong, even smart as we were to
learn the inevitability of a
weakness by witnessing
the natural course, taught to us
by the absence of our father.

Casual/Critical Encounters

Before internet personas and profile pages,
People would appear out of the dark.
If you knew them you'd build some working draft
of their outline in your imagination,
from what they'd shown you and
what you wanted to see.
People came around corners into you
like how on Seinfeld
each character was always
a riddle to be explained in caricature.
I think of this now at the park,
because I want to know the name of this tree
but it will die if I look it up on my phone,
its limbs its leaves
I must find a person
who can tell it to me.

Will Rogers

How the most important form of strength
is stamina,
life requiring a steady resilience
more than feats of excellence.
You trudge through and steer away from
and trust a steady step every once in awhile
when you need it. Flying out of the back door
of a bus onto a curb,
speaking up for what's right in casual conversation
without explosion
and trying your best over time
to recognize the low simmer of truth.

Forgive Me For Being Here

My friend once lived on a mattress on the floor
of an apartment inside a high-rise building in West Los
Angeles. I would
come over and we'd swim laps together
in the swimming pool of the building.
I saw an Ethan Hawke interview where
he said Linklater told him you don't have to go out
in search of life, that it's going to find you regardless.
The beauty then seems in our interpretations of it, life, this
unalterably extraordinary experience.
I'm in a coffee shop on that same street where my friend
once lived on the floor mattress,
and am thinking how the only way to understand our
connections to each other, God? The spirit web? Is to be
humbled again. To sleep on the floor,
in order to have access to the swimming pool.

Abalone Point Campground #2

The Japanese have the term "wabi sabi"
which means to find the holiness in imperfection.

But what of the already perfect? How must we define that
which makes our hearts swell? Continue beating in that
absolute blessed rhythm.

What of the wonder which colors our existence? Allows
our worries to evaporate? Locates the hidden symmetry
within?

The answer seems to be in surrendering to the question.
Saying, "I don't know how you found me but thank you.